WHAT TO DO NEXT

WHAT TO DO NEXT

SUE DYMOKE

Shoestring Press

All rights reserved. No part of this work covered by the copyright herein may be reproduced or used in any means – graphic, electronic, or mechanical, including copying, recording, taping, or information storage and retrieval systems – without written permission of the publisher.

Printed by imprintdigital
Upton Pyne, Exeter
www.digital.imprint.co.uk

Typesetting and cover design by The Book Typesetters
hello@thebooktypesetters.com
07422 598 168
www.thebooktypesetters.com

Published by Shoestring Press
19 Devonshire Avenue, Beeston, Nottingham, NG9 1BS
(0115) 925 1827
www.shoestringpress.co.uk

First published 2023
© Copyright: Sue Dymoke
© Cover photograph: David Belbin
© Author photograph: Graham Lester George

The moral right of the author has been asserted.

ISBN 978-1-915553-41-6

CONTENTS

Introduction   1

WHAT TO DO NEXT

Tapioca	15
Secret Girl	16
The Men in the Moon	17
Finds	18
Mobile	19
First Blood	20
Mischief along Cuckoo Lane	21
Biology	22
Becoming Silver Birch	23
Leaving Party	24
Hawk on the Window Ledge	25
Brass Bobbin Winders, 1914	26
Mending and Inspection, 1914	27
Drawing Lace, 1914	28
Our Bestwood Picnic	29
Wakes Outings	31
Questions for Postcard Photographers	33
Lost, Strayed or Stolen?	35
Sold	38
Flag-Staff	40
Ginger zinger	42
Galangin	45
Alcyonacea: Soft coral	46
Atomic dancers	47
DNA Time	48
Martin helps out on the allotment	52
At Cliff's Workshop	53
Unsolicited	54

Fast Anger	55
Green Alkanet	56
The sleepers in the hedge	57
Amelanchier	59
What befell them	60
Toad's Autumn Adventure	61
On Fire	62
The Camellia House	63
Holiday Village	65
Scopus Owl, Mallorca	66
Navigating half-sleep	67
Junior Sick Bay	68
Across Colne Water	69
November thanks	70
Out of time	71
Spring Learning	73
June '19 over Con-fusion	74
Raw country	76
When will the robin will come?	77
Hiding Places	78
Hitchers, Cuba	80
Staff-Student Committee Room, Autumn 1983	82
Wind wanderer	84
Instructions for a friend	85
Acknowledgements	87

INTRODUCTION

Sue assembled her fourth and final full collection of poetry less than two months before her death on June 13th, 2023. All of the poems she included were written following her breast cancer diagnosis in Spring, 2016, and the majority were written after secondary breast cancer was diagnosed in August, 2020, when she knew that she was terminally ill.

Sue was born in 1962 and grew up in Stevenage Old Town. Her parents were Jim, a joiner, who predeceased her by a little over eighteen months, aged 89, and Peggy, a former hairdresser and school dinner lady, who died of breast cancer when she was 52, in 1985. Sue wrote poems from an early age, inspired by the teaching of Letchmore Road Infant school's young headteacher, Rosemary Davis. Her first poem, which she collected in a pamphlet that she kept close to her writing desk, was about mankind landing on the moon in 1969.

Teachers were very important in Sue's life when she was growing up. Her other great inspiration was Richard Wallace, at the Barclay School in Stevenage Old Town, who became a lifelong friend, encouraging her reading and writing. She published many poems in the school magazine. Her poetry fell away while she was doing her English Literature degree at the University of Nottingham from 1980 to 1983, where her experience was more mixed. But she loved her 1983–4 English PGCE (Post-graduate certificate of Education) course.

This was when we met, an encounter partly described in the poem, 'Staff-Student Committee Room', which she chose to include here, one of many she wrote for the 39 anniversaries of the day I persuaded her to go out with me. She thought that I was too old (four years her senior), too arrogant and too brazenly left wing. Nevertheless we had a great deal in common, not least our love of good writing. Our first date was a reading by the poet Peter Porter, who would later become a friend. Sue graduated with distinction and took a job at Dayncourt

Comprehensive, Radcliffe-on-Trent, which had a mix of middle class and mining families. She moved into my rented Radford terrace. A few months later we bought a two-bedroom terrace with a tiny garden in nearby Bobbers Mill, Nottingham.

We'd tried writing stories for children together at the end of the PGCE course, and now each began to write in earnest, reading and commenting on each other's work. Sue's poetry took off in summer 1986, when she attended an Arvon course with the poets Ian McMillan and John Latham. Ian encouraged Sue to submit to magazines. Soon she began to be published in journals like *The North* and *Iron*. She became an honorary member of the Huddersfield poetry scene, attending and, later, giving workshops at the Poetry Business in Huddersfield. *The Wide Skirt* press published her first pamphlet *A Sort of Clingfilm* in 1987, and this was closely followed by a joint Smith Doorstop pamphlet with Clare Chapman, *Colour Girl*, in 1988. The first reading she gave was with another young poet who emerged from the same scene, Simon Armitage. Both had pamphlets published by our friend John Harvey's *Slow Dancer* Press. Sue was the British Poetry editor of the *Slow Dancer* journal for some years.

In 1990, my first novel came out and I quit teaching full time, while Sue left Dayncourt for West Bridgford School, where, at 29, she became the youngest head of English in the county. She kept writing but the job did fully absorb Sue, who gave her all to the students and colleagues she mentored. We bought our house in Sherwood with a larger garden (and, later, the allotment behind it, which we restored and Sue tended lovingly) in 1994. In the second half of the nineties, we formed close friendships with our neighbour, the novelist Stanley Middleton (and his wife Margaret, with whom Sue shared a passion for gardening) and the poet, professor, critic and jazzman John Lucas, whose Shoestring Press published Sue's first full collection, *The New Girls*, in 2002.

Sue was determinedly ambitious. Given her mother's early death and that of her aunt, Nan, at 64, also from breast cancer, she always suspected that her own time might be cut short. Toward the end of the 90s, she began to apply for deputy headships and got interviews, but her heart wasn't in it. Encouraged by Professor Bernard Harrison in Sheffield, she undertook a PhD on what had become her most passionate academic interest, 'The Teaching of Poetry in Secondary Schools'. Many teachers were scared of teaching poetry, even more so of writing it, and students were often encouraged to see poems as puzzles rather than enriching works of art. Sue wanted to show that poetry was for everyone. In 1999 she took unpaid leave from school teaching and never returned. That year she was awarded a schoolteacher fellowship at Sidney Sussex College, Cambridge, an honour which our friend Stanley Middleton had also received at the end of his teaching career. Like him, she attended lectures on the romantics by the modernist poet J.H. Prynne. She also formed a firm friendship with another schoolteacher fellow, Gary Snapper, who would soon become a close colleague, and his new partner (now husband), scientist and poet Pietro Roversi, with whom Sue was to collaborate on the poem, 'DNA Time', included here.

Sue received her PhD from the University of Nottingham and, rather than return to teaching, took up temporary lecturing jobs there and at The Open University. In 2001 she became publications officer for NATE (the National Association for the Teaching of English, which she had long been a keen member of) where she worked closely with Gary, who would become editor of NATE's *Teaching English* journal, to which Sue would regularly contribute.

In 2003 she found the kind of job she'd long been after when she was appointed to run the English PGCE at the University of Leicester. She was promoted to Reader in Education and went on to lead the PGCE course. These were productive years, in which Sue wrote much poetry and did the groundbreaking research which made her so influential in and beyond the world of poetry in education. Her book *Drafting and Assessing Poetry* was a seminal work, while the *Poetry Matters* series (with Andrew

Lambirth and Anthony Wilson) explored the contemporary status of poetry teaching in schools and proposed ways forward. The series resulted in two influential publications, *Making Poetry Matter: International Research on Poetry Pedagogy* and *Making Poetry Happen: Transforming the Poetry Classroom* (Bloomsbury 2013).

Sue loved her time as a Visiting Scholar at the University of Auckland in 2011, and returned to New Zealand twice, the second time with me, looked after by her close friend Ngaire Hoben and family. The same year she was awarded a National Teaching Fellowship in recognition of her work on poetry. Five years later, Sue gave the Harold Rosen memorial lecture (with her Primary School headteacher, Rosemary Davis, now CBE, in attendance). In it, she drew on her own personal experiences at school and in her later career – linking these with the seminal work of Harold Rosen and John Dixon on personal growth – in order to illustrate the ways in which teachers can empower children from all backgrounds through language and literature. Her recurring argument was that at the centre of teaching poetry should be students *writing* their own poetry. In 2017 Sue was presented with the NATE award for Outstanding Contribution to Research. Sue was also a board member of UKLA (literacy association), First Story (encouraging young writers) and NAWE (writing in Education) to all of which she made significant contributions. The *Young Poets' Stories* project (in collaboration with Anthony Wilson and the Foyle Young Poet of the Year awards) had a strong impact on the young poets she worked with and the book documenting the research will be published in 2024. The best way to understand Sue's story and how it fed her philosophy of poetry teaching is by reading her own words. I recommend the Harold Rosen lecture, *It All Began with the Moon: Finding and Keeping Poetry**, which can be found on Sue's website and in issue 12 of the journal *Teaching English*.

---

* https://suedymokepoetry.files.wordpress.com/2021/06/nate_te_issue-12_27-32.pdf

In spring 2016, Sue was diagnosed with breast cancer. By now, the BRCA gene had been discovered. She eventually underwent an expensive test to determine whether her cancer was caused by a defective gene. It was. She had multiple debilitating treatments and operations to remove the cancer and reduce the risk. Even so, we knew it was likely to return. During the brief period when Sue was told that she was cancer free (although this turned out not to be the case) she applied for and was appointed to an Associate Professorship in Education at Nottingham Trent University, on a fast track to a full professorship. We worked, briefly, in opposite buildings (I have held a part time Creative Writing lectureship at NTU since 2002). Her work was already well known and respected at NTU. She brought excitement to her new department, which she loved. Then came the Covid pandemic and Sue, because of her cancer history, was deemed clinically vulnerable. She was severely circumscribed by having to shield. In August 2020, during a break between lockdowns, she was told that she had secondary breast cancer. A blurred image in her spine, which had been too vague to assess at the end of her previous treatment, was now diagnosed as a tumour.

Consultants advised that treatments might extend her life by several years. She was encouraged to live her life as fully as possible. Sue chose to continue doing the work she loved. The first treatment worked for a year, then she moved on to a less effective one. When that ceased to be effective, she was put on a different course of treatment that, we were to discover, barely worked at all. The first signs of the stomach tumour that killed her appeared while we were on holiday in Bergen, Norway, in August 2022, although it was only diagnosed seven days before her death in June 2023.

During those seven years of illness, Sue continued to write, to travel (in particular, to Hiroshima, where she gave several lectures and workshops, working with Yuka Nakai, whose own PhD was partly about Sue's work). Sue was an enthusiastic, ambitious chef who loved to entertain and kept doing so. We designed and had built a new summer-house-cum-shed on our allotment. Right up to the very end of her life, Sue saw as many films, plays, dance events and concerts as she could fit in. Her particular passions were jazz and world music. We made many trips to the Nottingham jazz club, *Peggy's Skylight*, which opened in 2018, and saw the Senegalese kora player, Seckou Keita, several times. His was the last CD she bought. She would have been thrilled to know that Peggy's House band and Seckou Keita agreed to perform at her memorial celebration, which takes place on the same day that this book is published, November 5th, 2023.

Sue's final illness was at first blamed on a stricture in the oesophagus but an operation made it no easier for her to swallow or keep food down. We both knew that the problem might be something more serious. She lost a lot of weight. Nevertheless, she kept writing and teaching. We cancelled two trips but Sue felt strong enough for us to take a week's holiday in Malta with her oldest friend, Tracy Farish, and Tracy's husband Greg only a few weeks before she died. There, we visited the hypogeum, the Caravaggios in St John's Co-Cathedral in Valetta and, although she was by now very weak, made a day trip to Gozo on our last full day. Evelyn Gibbs' painting of the salt pans there has hung in our dining room for 25 years and we were both keen to see where it was painted. The tour bus needed to get petrol so we had an extra twenty minutes to wander round on our own. The photo on the cover of this book (like her previous two Shoestring covers, an iPhone photo, but this time taken by me) shows some of those salt pans and, in the distance, Sue exploring.

The weekend before she went into hospital, Sue insisted on our watching a new print of her favourite movie, Bill Forsyth's *Local Hero*. The Monday was a bank holiday, and, although she was starting to fade, she was alert enough to enjoy and discuss the final episode of the TV series *Succession*. Once in hospital, however, she declined rapidly. The doctors were able to stabilise her and, a week later, operated to put stents in her throat and stomach to help her digest food. That was when they found the large tumour in her stomach which had been impossible to diagnose without surgery. At that point, the only options remaining were desperate and offered little quality of life, so Sue made the decision to die at home.

She had squeezed every drop of joy she could from life, and still wasn't finished. The following day, while I was getting the house ready and waiting for a hospital bed to be delivered, Sue and Tracy organised for us to have a civil partnership by special license in our garden. This we did, two days later, with Tracy and Greg as witnesses, and our old friend Rob Wetheridge as celebrant, surrounded by close family and twenty or so friends who lived nearby. The ceremony took place in glorious sunshine, under a pergola that Sue's brother Dave and nephew Harry, master carpenters, had constructed the day before. Her nephew Michael handed us our wedding rings, which had belonged to Sue's mother, grandmother and brother (who, luckily for me, had a spare). For her wedding vow, Sue read a poem that she had written for and about me some fifteen years earlier.

DIGGING PARSNIPS
(for Dave, November 2008)

We are digging parsnips in the dark
you and me
twenty five years after our first autumn.

We are digging – not picking – parsnips in the dark
you and me.
You, uncertain as ever about which leaves
or spot of damp earth you should be looking at,
hold the torch and cast
not quite enough light in the wrong place.
Your mind is focused on a late goal or
a rare book film plot twist

download CD gig ticket on the horizon.
But only slightly focused
because you do want to eat those
small sweet parsnips and
because, with a call or two or three,
you're back here again with me
digging parsnips
always.

That was on Friday. On Saturday afternoon, she told me that she'd chosen the title for this collection: *What To Do Next*. That evening she was trying to write a poem and asked me to look up the meaning of the word *lodestar*. Later, when she woke in the night, she reminded me that she'd chosen a title, and I repeated it to her. We didn't discuss the title, but it made complete sense to me, suggesting the determined optimism with which she lived her life and the dark humour which allowed her to face the inevitable. It is also the question she has left me with.

'I love you so. I'm happy I ended my life with a poem. I'm happy,' were her last words before she went back to sleep at three in the morning. She had used up all her strength and lost consciousness completely the following evening. Thirty-six hours later she died.

Meeting Sue and being loved by her has been the greatest luck of my life. Many others shared that luck. The tributes to Sue were overwhelming, as were the condolence cards I received, making clear the enormous impact she had on so many people. Teacher Chris Hildrew spoke for many when he wrote: 'I was fortunate enough to meet and work with Sue as part of the English PGCE network in Nottinghamshire. She encouraged a generation of English teachers to be creative, bold and brave. Her legacy lives in the countless lives she has touched and enriched.' On social media, The Poetry Society posted: 'Poetry has lost one of its finest champions. We will miss Sue Dymoke immeasurably.' Sue's friend Jackie Kay, who had a residency at West Bridgford school in the 90s and sent her long, lovely phone messages on the last weekend of her life, posted: 'Loved Sue Dymoke – she taught me so much & all her pupils loved her. I remember those residencies back at West Bridgford, early 90s vividly & all the times at yours with the amazing Sue-chef food... she will be so missed by so many who loved her.'

Our close friend David Almond wrote Sue's obituary for *The Guardian*. His beautiful piece was illustrated by the lovely photograph which is also on the back cover of this collection. Our friend Graham Lester George snatched it at the table on the patio between our house and garden.

Sue bequeathed a generous sum to the Poetry Society and this will support the development of new generations of young poets. The society's director, Judith Palmer, wrote: 'All the work we do in the education department is already in a way part of her legacy – we've all benefitted so much from the work she did to promote writing for young people.'

*

The poems in this collection find Sue revisiting some familiar ground but also pushing forward in new directions. They fall into several groups. A number arise from the Poetry Place project that Sue instigated with *Inspire* (Nottinghamshire libraries) through the *Miner2Major* scheme and workshops conducted online during the pandemic, with work emerging from images that Sue carefully selected from the online Inspire Picture Archive. In the introduction to the 2021 book of Poetry Place (which includes many of the photographs – some of which are reproduced in the following pages – and poems from workshop members) Sue wrote that the project 'stemmed from my long-held interests in taking and viewing photographs and exploring local archives. I have a firm belief that unexpected discoveries can inspire writing.' The exhibition has been extended and, at the time of publication, can be seen at Nottingham's historic Bromley House Library (which Sue and I joined more than 25 years ago), where it is dedicated to Sue's memory. The exhibition (with the photos that inspired the poems and the poems by participants) can also be viewed online.*

Sue and I were heavily involved with 2015's successful bid for Nottingham to become a UNESCO City of Literature. She held a virtual residency in Melbourne during the pandemic, writing, researching and leading UNESCO workshops. Some of the 'found' poems that Sue loved to play around with are included here and, like the Poetry Place poems, show what gold she could mine by exploring archives.

There are a number of poems that stem from childhood memories of Stevenage Old Town, such as 'Secret Girl' and 'Men in the Moon', which revisits the event that inspired Sue's first poem, written when she was seven. Two poems were written for online 70th birthday festschrifts for old friends, the poets Martin Stannard and Cliff Yates. Some poems deal with our travels, to Mallorca, Cuba, Norfolk, France and, closer to home, the Camellia House in Wollaton Park.

Several poems reference science, which Sue was always interested to discuss with friends who knew more than she did. The most recent is a collaboration with Stephen Wren, which he kindly allowed me to include. He introduces it here, while Pietro Roversi has fashioned the introduction to 'DNA Time', the shape poem which was also the subject of a 2019 Radio Four documentary *Recombinant Rhymes and DNA Art*. At the time of writing, this is still available from the BBC online.

Other poems reference the pandemic and teaching on the 'Teams' app during this terrible time. The two love poems Sue chose to include detail the start of our relationship in 1983 and a 2019 break we took in France, staying at our friends Stephen and Tanya's remote farmhouse, surrounded by acres of wild land, during the year when we thought Sue was cancer-free. The last poem speaks for itself.

---

* https://www.inspireculture.org.uk/reading-information/reading/poetryplace-online-exhibition/

The poems that Sue sent to John Lucas in April were not ordered for a collection and did not include the collaborative poems or a handful of others (for instance, a good example of her children's poetry) which John and I felt it was useful to collect. Therefore the order and final form in which they appear was my decision, with advice from John but inspired, I hope, by a firm understanding and empathy for the way in which Sue worked. We were, throughout our adult lives, close collaborators as well as beloved partners, showing each other work first and trusting each other's instincts about what needed cutting, what needed sharpening, what needed moving to a more effective place. Without her in my life, a large part of me is missing. It's some comfort to have her present in these poems, which complete a passionately lived life and a fully achieved career as a writer, researcher, teacher and fierce advocate for the power of poetry.

David Belbin

What To Do Next

TAPIOCA
(for Peter Kahn)

Huge aluminium tureens clank
splashing in and out of sinks.
Dinner ladies clatter and
clear, chatter and laugh
wash and unwind.
Shutters are shutting down
canteen serving hatches wince
their way to sturdy closure.
Half full water jugs are emptied,
plastic cups in fading primary colours
stacked, cutlery sorted and stored.
Here, in wiped-clean silent space,
I remain with one other refuser.

Don't waste it. Eat it up NOW!
Get it down.
You can't leave until it's all gone.
It's good for you.

Shiny milk frogspawn
tepid, growing cold
congeals colder while dinner time
stretches into end of playtime,
late afternoon, nearly home time.
The bowl stares back at me.

SECRET GIRL

Gliding down the climbing frame
Janice spins inside her yellow hoop
cradles family secrets
among screaming playground grey.

Janice breaks up birch twigs
peels and counts the waxy pieces.
If their number's even
the devil will catch you soon.

Janice says laburnum weeps
deadly evil poisonous tears.
She sidles through switch grass
by our big red classroom wall.

Janice finds my dinner coins
stashed beneath shining conkers.
She won't say who took them
but they know that she knows.

Janice is a Russian doll
a house with hiding places
a face behind the mirror
and a diamond among glass.

Janice with the ice blond stare
rides her grandad's fairground pony
blue cape flaring out
North wind streaming through her hair.

THE MEN IN THE MOON

The day before the Eagle lands
we walk home up Letchmore Road
from Deni's 7th birthday party,
me clutching a piece of cake,
Dad wheeling his bike.
Above rooftops,
through the railings of our tarmacked schoolyard
the Moon's saucer glows.

My questions start,
ones I'd wanted to ask for ages
but sounded too daft for the classroom.
Will I see the astronauts up there?
Will their flagpole stick out in the night sky?
Will the Stars and Stripes flutter in the wind?
Will they meet the Man in the Moon?

Dad smiles his laughing smile,
says That Old Man is bigger than them
and, anyway, they might not land in the right place
but if, they did, he might give them a piece of cheese.

The next day bubble-headed Armstrong
and Aldrin step out in huge shiny-white suits
onto a lonely, cratered surface.
I stare up from our dark garden,
imagine their bleeping capsule
see footprints, showers of Moon dust,
the Man in the Moon grinning
at two men bouncing, far away.

FINDS

He was always digging up flints
splitting nails on his splintered fingers
in garden borders or vegetable beds
or one of two allotments that frayed
mum's temper, kept him out of the house.

In pretend excavations Dave
and I longed to discover spearheads
knapped to fine points
ammonites or dinosaur teeth.
Instead, beneath the lilac we unearthed
an *ivory* bracelet of pre-war Bakelite
an *ancient* snake belt buckle
a tiny silver coin we buffed
to a semi-shine with vinegar
took to a dealer on Albert Street.

It was not Roman.

MOBILE

She taps out a number with electronic bleeps
lets someone know she'll be late
for an interview she would have made
with half an hour to spare

were circumstances different for her
different for the soul who threw their life on the track
different for us
stranded
losing our reservations
our Supersaver days out
reduced to afternoon excursions
while the train crawls and mobiles trill.

On the way home she's at it again
beyond Wellingborough and Kettering
into Leicester and Loughborough
cutting through whining children
and waves of tiredness
she dips into her buzzing handbag
talks of her smiling chauffeur
the warm bath she longs for
then puts us out of one misery
into another
with her account
of the burnt brakes
stinking out our carriage.

FIRST BLOOD

Podding peas in the dregs of August
when blood came warm and strange.

I would be bound up for years
lose a week every month, they said.

Even then truth was muddled by pain
and what they hoped I'd learned in school.

From that point there were no more reassurances:
no going back.

MISCHIEF ALONG CUCKOO LANE

The first time we heard about muntjacs
we thought they were a joke.
Scales Park, third year Primary
out on the hunt with Mrs James
listening to bluebells, searching for sting-free nettles,
we found earthworms, insects lurking in rotting timbers
sketched them on rough paper before
they scurried away from magnified eyes.

Rabbits were old school
we saw plenty, heard lesser spotteds
hammering on birch
picked primrose, red campion, shepherd's purse
late spring for pressing
but a muntjac, safari park escapee turned wild
short-arsed deer with lonely habits
and prone to barking:
that was the beast to be seen.

Before the coach came, our class watched
for undergrowth movement.
A clearing ringed with curious children
would have been enough to send
any mammal into deep cover.
No muntjacs, not that time.

Years later in gathering owl dusk
a sturdy stunted ungulate pushes
through hedge banks thick with cow parsley
gambols away from yelping dogs
to ransack flowerbeds, a veg patch or two
cause more mischief along Cuckoo Lane
no time for sightseers.

BIOLOGY

She liked to categorise.
On the first day of my first term
she mistook me for the school villain's sister.
No apology and
I never forgave her.

Fierce in steel-rimmed glasses
she stifled all our questions
her tongue sharper
than an incision.

In her neat lab biology
was reduced to a blackboard
crawling with clever Latin
prepared in advance for us to copy.

BECOMING SILVER BIRCH

becoming Silver Birch
you shape your limbs to the
supple
    trunk
bends

    slip in
and out
    of bark
sleeving yourself in second skin
white through woodland dark
in a faraway summer

your arms touch inwards
                        awkward

plait turns astray

you are drawn inside yourself
rooted

LEAVING PARTY

Swallows punctuate the day:
their blue-black bodies string an ellipsis
across wires of a warm October sky:
Our air will cool soon and they know it.

In one final fling, they begin
to dip and dazzle, thresh and turn
skim tops of horse chestnuts and limes
snatch their insect buffet on the wing.

In one enormous shoal they plummet
the depths of windscreens far beneath,
rise up and away from dark
afternoons and winter pickings.

In one last swoop their forked tails
flash against the light   are gone.

HAWK ON THE WINDOW LEDGE

Five minutes before a storm
the headland blazes in early morning and
our room floods with Lizard light.
Inches away, beyond glass
a young hawk preens himself on the ledge
oblivious to kettle steam or radio babble
combs curved beak through breast plumage
checks with steely eyes
teases every feather to optimum flight potential.
Later he will return to play with baby crows
try to snatch one in mid air.
Now he angles and throws his body skyward
glides then hovers without motion
scans bracken ready to drop
in one last second of clarity
before a storm-bludgeoned sea
steals the vanishing shoreline.

BRASS BOBBIN WINDERS, 1914

Talking is never easy
amid machine pull and purr
clank and yank
among serried ranks of bent heads
with only other people's backs to speak to.
Mrs Shepherd with her rounded shoulders
Mrs Albone's slight frame
obscured by heavy folds, ruffled sleeves
Mr North's straight white-aproned spine
Mrs Furr, sitting higher than the rest
thanks to a thick plank
on top of her three-legged stool.

Cottons move
reel to reel
spool to spool
black on black
white on white.
Thick tight straps
run ceiling-wards
drive spindles
create row on row
stack on stack
bobbins primed for action.

MENDING AND INSPECTION, 1914

In this cramped space
windows are tipped wide open.
Thirty-six women, hair pinned,
brooches at throats, bow
to shrouds of lace
clasped in silent devotion.

Hardened fingers tease needles
through invisible tears in thread, send
fine fabric pouring down laps and knees
past carefully tucked-in boots to pool
in slippery twists across the stone floor.

At prayer, no-one talks or smiles
or moves from their creaky stools
except with upmost caution.

Eyes, necks, backs
strain, ache, stiffen
in the long afternoon
before shift end.

Then light steals away
and the stern ones
inspect all their handiwork.

DRAWING LACE, 1914

On sunny side streets or sweltering top floors
girls aged ten to sixteen tilt forward
on benches, ankles crossed
smocked aprons or pinafores
over regular clothes.

Some stand, hoping for
greater comfort while they toil.
Most stoop over strips
slipping through their fingers
into wicker baskets between their feet.

Their eyes trace lace edges
passing through each handspan
draw out long threads, hold them together
clip away stray cottons to reveal
patterns beneath

one inch breadths destined for
curtains, table cloths and antimacassars
scalloped collars, fine gloves and hat veils
the like of which
they'll never wear.

OUR BESTWOOD PICNIC
Bestwood Village Children's Picnic Bulwell, c 1910

We were a bright blaze
in that picture you took.
You capture our closeness, hesitant curiosity
sisters, cousins lapping up sunshine
on a rare half day for whole families.
Pinafores pressed, boaters brushed
best Sunday hats entwined with roses.
You can't see the pink and lilac ribbons
picked by our mams for the outing.
Boys dapper in waistcoats, crisp white sleeves.
Bare legs spread, mams hoping
the grass won't stain
give them yet more washing.

Always copper steam
dolly pounding in our house
scalding water, banished dust, sweat.

Always dust, settling deep in seams
daily after each shift, skins ingrained
elbows, necks, forearms, fingers
darkest black, reaching deep.

Nettle raises your hand to mimic your actions
takes her imaginary photograph.
Some of us are barefooted
ready for another runaround
after all this waiting.
Some of us are blurred, whited out
others more or less invisible.

Annie holds her tea cup steady
while you count down a frozen minute
our fixed stares straining smiles.
Flo is all grown up, guarding our wicker basket
covered with a cotton cloth to stop flies
in the unexpected heat.

What were we eating that day
a bit more than our usual snap?
Joseph was tucking into his ginger cake
when you rolled up
and nothing was going to stop him.
Mabel was anxious, tried to hold her baby sister still
even though she would not face the front
more interested in the hurdy-gurdy man just out of frame.

WAKES OUTINGS

Yours are Shetland ponies
like we've never seen
suspended from poles
eyes shining alert
nostrils flaring in grassy air
tails brushed, coats gleaming
in readiness for another sedate spin
to nowhere, solo or in pairs
pulling fancy carriages fit for Sundays
to the slow turn of your showman's reel

Your fairground gallopers are the only ones
being driven today, Mr Miles.
We, scrubbed up in our straw boaters,
wave at twirling Annie and Jean.
Mam keeps her eye on gurgling Lou
holds a shawl in case of sudden chill
tries to enjoy us all together for once
first day of Wakes
days without darkness, without fear.

Yours are the only ponies working today, Mr Miles
Others blink their way overground
for once-a-year daylight
breezes to ruffle their manes
soft pasture and skylarks
rest and freshness.
Jess and Bessy whinny their
heads off in open fields
away from grind and noise
narrowness

away from low light and heat
harshness
until a juddering lift calls us
back below
to fill and haul the tubs
coal face to flats
flats to coal face
underground.

QUESTIONS FOR POSTCARD PHOTOGRAPHERS
Nottinghamshire 1912

Where do you wander?
Are you on foot or cycling?
Are you laden or travelling light
new box brownie in your canvas bag?
What makes you stop, measure
with your shutter-shaped hands
hold that frame in your mind?

You ticked off all the famous sights months ago
Bosun's Grave, Budby Castle, King John's Palace.
You've had your fill of Lodges and Halls countywide
and everybody's taken enough shots of the Ancient Oak
shored and propped, trunk split open
just enough for visitors to slip inside, if slender.

So what's next? How much could you get
for that public house, lintel gate or village memorial?
The fire from Morley's Smithy or a drover urging
his cows to parlour along Baulker Lane?
Maypole dancers twisting ribbons
on a spring green or that new-fangled tractor
soon to usurp Black Hills' horse-drawn ways?
Twelve-year-old pinafored girls
their last school afternoon before service beckons
a gathering of Sunday bonnets, pull of oars,
a solitary fisherman at Thoresby Lake,
Edwinstowe fielder hunched
for a catch that never comes?

What happens when scenes
are filled with grime, sweat and desperation?
Coal picked and gathered
into pail, sack, barrow
Coal dust on every whisker, pore and cuticle.
Shirt sleeves rolled, men's faces
caught in grimacing smiles
uncertain how they should look
while their women, boys, whole families
scour slag heaps
in the chill spring nights.

Do you ever ask for names, stories, reasons?
Or are they just another day's record
fixed on postcard paper, sold at a village counter
bought in a hurry, dashed off with a pencilled message
"Nan sends love, back by 6 tomorrow"
postage paid.

LOST, STRAYED OR STOLEN?

(found in advertisements and articles from: The Melbourne Advertiser, 1838; The Melbourne Argus, 1846 and The Melbourne Daily News, 1848–1851)

Between Melbourne and the Ford
of the Salt Water River, 17th Decm last
a Lady's handsome Gold Ear Drop.
Whoever will bring the lost Earring
to the Office of this paper
shall be handsomely rewarded.

On the Keilor road
evening of Tuesday, the 20th Instant
the reel of a fishing rod, with hair line attached.

The fine new Schooner *Squatter* (total loss).

A Butcher's pass book
any person having found the same
will receive a liberal reward
if produced without delay
to R. Bust, Butcher, Elisabeth Street
opposite the post office.

From Pentridge, on the 8th ultimo
a chestnut horse
white star in the forehead
bearing a switch tail.

Job Chatterley, a potter by trade,
absconded from our hired service
Chenery and Goodman,
Delatite, Devils River, 27th June 1846.

A pocket book
containing UK register of the Schooner *Margaret*
and sundry other papers.

One light iron grey mare,
Lg scar above her off flank.
two pounds if strayed
four pounds if stolen.

On or about the 8th instant
between Mr Patterson's station,
Edward River, and the Sir Walter Scott Inn
an order drawn by Mr William Patterson
in favour of William Forest
dated 9th February 1851 of £9.
Payment of this order has been STOPPED.

On Thursday evening last
in the vicinity of Dandenong,
a dark brown pocket book with a steel spring
containing a number of promissory notes.

The Mailbag containing letters and newspapers
for distribution along the road
between Melbourne and Ballan
having been lost by the mail-man
between Saltwater Pound
and Mr. Solomon's station
about a mile from the latter place.

A Bay colt
blaze in face
last seen at Bacchus Marsh.
Lost – supposed to be stolen. On Sunday afternoon from St Kilda.
A small black and white spaniel dog –

King Charles Breed –
has lost an eye
walks rather lame.

Ten Guineas Reward
Whereas a child, three years of age,
son of Mr W.M. of the South Yarra Pound
wandered from his father's house
on the morning of Thursday last
has not since been seen or heard of.

The lighthouse
fixed by Mr Bush on the Goodwin Sands
has disappeared.

SOLD
(from The Melbourne Argus, Fri 3rd Jul 1846)

9 dozen oval plates
ditto soup, ditto creams
ewers, basins, chambers
raw and boiled oils

Stout grey sheeting
fine white shirting
Brussels carpeting
superior Barnsley drill

Monkey, pea and reefer jackets
drab moleskin and velveteens
fancy plaid vestings
and Cosban shalloons

Check, striped and harness book
36 in soft white duck
Adelaide and bird-eye gimps
printed llama shawls

Table rice, allspice
pepper and liquorice
annatto, chrome yellow
Prussian, thumb blue

Volatile salts and isinglass
brimstone and sulphur
bottled fruits and salad oils
hard and soft soap

Grocer's paper
Chemist's paper
faint lines and note paper
carraway, canary and garden seeds

15 quiet broken in cows
in calf and with young calves
ditto 9 heifers
ditto young steers

FLAG-STAFF

The Melbourne Daily News
Dec 27th, 1851, page 3

Dec 1st, 2021

Flag-Staff Inn provides
an intimate situation too well
   known
to require any further
   observation

a well-placed most conducive
   spot
for you to take a break
from your busy days

no exertions shall be wanting

not too far from the city centre

a haven of rest and relaxation
just steps away
from the numerous attractions

pure air, delightful scenery
a retired locality within a few
   minutes
stroll the heart of the city

many facilities to enrich your
   stay

no trifling advantages

home to 6 bedrooms, all
tastefully furnished many
even provide such comforts as
television LCD/plasma screen

meets the wishes of all classes
all the comforts, the tastes of all
without fear of interruption

no stone left unturned

very good as far as noise goes

all parties share substantial
   inducements
secure bullock yards, good
   stabling
well aired-bedrooms

guests can enjoy on-site
   features
laundromat, 24-hour front
   desk
free Wi-Fi in all rooms!

no pains spared

carpeting, cleaning products

the prospect of uninterrupted
   health
the absolute certainty
of a return to convalescence

no exertions shall be wanting

the very best accommodation
a well-lined larder for man
   and beast
may be depended upon

one trial will prove it deserving
all the praise

complimentary instant coffee
complimentary tea
will offer total renewal.

facilities for disabled guests

the hotel's gardens are ideal
   places
to relax and unwind
after a busy day

whatever your purpose of visit
an excellent choice for your
   stay

GINGER ZINGER

Fibrous rhizome
ginger zinger
brings zip and tingle
to palate and plate

Fresh ginger houses gingerol
(the strong antioxidant):

[structure of gingerol, with HO– and –OCH₃ on the aromatic ring, and a side chain containing a ketone (O) and a hydroxyl (OH)]

Masking marine tastes
mashing for medicines
ginger for digestion
ensures comfort and cure

Lashings and lashings
of ginger beer picnics
fizz and tang of Jamaica
on a balmy summer's day

When cooked, it becomes
zingerone (spicy and sweet):

[structure of zingerone, with HO– and –O– (methoxy) on the aromatic ring, and a side chain with a ketone]

Parlies and parkin
tharf carke and fairings
Ormskirk dark and Grasmere
or tasty Ashbourne white

Ginger nuts and pfeffernüsse
lebkuchen and speculaas
ginger men stepping out
with iced white smiles

Gari for sushi, Shoga buds for
tofu and tempura
soups and sashimi
but not for forgetfulness

Dried ginger loses water
(gingerol forms shogaol):

Ginger tea from Kashmir
ginger ale for whisky
ginger green, ginger dried
ginger pickled and preserved

Ginger steeped in Sanskrit
handed down from troglodytes
crossing Pfefferlander
through Persia, Greece and Rome

Knobbled and noded
knarled and budded
a thunder for the tongue
a wonder for the nose

Sue Dymoke and Stephen Paul Wren

This poem was published shortly after Sue's death (alongside 'Biology') in the journal *Dreich*. Stephen Wren writes 'Sue and I decided to collaborate on a poem that spoke to the chemistry and properties of ginger as part of facebook group *Molecules Unlimited* (Sue was an important contributor to this community). I identified some key chemical components of ginger whilst Sue focussed on the properties/uses of ginger (from global sources). We then combined these strands into an educational poem about the subject.'

GALANGIN

A molecular astronaut from station Flavonol
you probe disease space
infiltrate enemy cells
force their retreat.
You buzz with anti-bacterial
anti-viral activity.

Hope
resOnates
thrOugH
your
honey hive.

ALCYONACEA: SOFT CORAL
(Partial source: healthcare.utah.edu press release, May 2022)

Rare soft coral
colonises in reef systems
is made to be eaten
not destined for jeweller's hands

unleashes Eleutherobin
disrupts the cytoskeleton
breaks down scaffolds
defends itself against predators.

She lurks in secret waters
but to reconstruct her compound
and piece together her code
scientists dive fathoms deep into DNA dark
—
scan cookery books for an unreadable recipe
impenetrable manuscripts for a musical score
seek the opening to a secret tomb
with no map to guide them.

To programme created bacteria
after all that searching
they must follow alyconacea's instructions.
Only then can they take first steps

from ocean
to lab bench
to bedside blister pack.

ATOMIC DANCERS

Bright
movers,
sparking steel
ball-bearings ricochet across
irregular pockets of velvet space
and skin, blood and bone, air and fire,
stone and water. Intuitive salsa partners synced in unending live sequences, test out
question, ponder, probe outer limits, spin their polished spheres around what is known,
what is hoped, what is yet to know.

DNA TIME

"The chain twists, spirals, shapes each destiny differently, translates lives as rare, certain, less defined."

Sue's strand of *DNA Time* encodes her protein poem, above. She elaborated on the poem's genesis on *Recombinant Rhymes and DNA Art*, a BBC Radio 4 broadcast about DNA Time:

"I come from a family with a history of breast cancer and succumbed to the disease several years ago. During the process of my treatment I became very interested in exploring the actual structure of what was happening to me inside and the science of it and being able to kind of name the things that were going on. I have been a friend of Pietro's for a long long time and we both talked about poetry and he and a number of other scientist friends started to explain things to me in ways that had not been explained to me before. That developed my curiosity about the language and the structures of DNA and that's where our conversation started really."

"There was quite a difficult period when I misinterpreted Pietro's rules and I spent about two days working solidly on a version of my poem and very proudly sent it to him and said: "There are no Bs no Js no Us no Xs nor Zs in this poem!" and he E-mailed me back within half an hour and said: "Ah – ehm – you could have put those letters in, Sue." And I screamed a lot – and started again on another version the next day."

Pietro Roversi adds: "Sue and I started to have conversations about the molecular basis of inheritance and cancer. Those conversations developed her curiosity about the language and the structure of DNA. When I mentioned one can write text with "DNA constraints" she came up with the idea of the collaborative project that became *DNA Time*. Writing *DNA*

Time not only enabled Sue to concentrate fully on writing new poetry during a very challenging period of ill health and intensive treatment but it also led to the deepening of her understanding of nucleic acid structures and their beauty. On my part, I had a chance to explore the impact of DNA from a broader perspective rather than a purely molecular one. Last, but not least, the poem(s) triggered discussions with Sue's doctors and other scientist friends who had not previously considered fusing poetry and DNA translation and were intrigued by the scientific precision of our writing processes."

Sue Dymoke & Pietro Roversi

All child time contained patterned acts
foreign, rare, franked stamps, hinged commemoratives
catalogued according to Gibbons
scales practised daily
tiny skyscraps arranged, jigsaw corners searched and selected
mammal tracks magnified, golden leaves traced
petals sought, picked, flattened beneath encyclopaedias.
Spirograph created intricate images
felt-tip colours and Caran d'ache pencils
shaded within margins
early evening battleships, draughts,
chessmen, chinese chequers threatened
plastic counters crept along ladders
avoiding gigantic coiled snakes
continuous knitting clicked
lengthening scarves, v-necks, cardigans.

What a great
excitement blooming fast, springing into the matrix
nurturing perfect youth! Cuddle, travel,
dance, grow beautiful/handsome, touch happiness
consciously, chase tangible dreams, grasp the magic
liberating efforts that turn children
into accomplished grown-ups! Pretend this perfection
lasts, sail again and again along
happy ascending currents that throughout childhood
remained covert and finally stand strong.
Affirm, expand, project. Gain, generate, protect.
Maximise feelings and thoughts, listen, touch;
remembering won't recreate, recalling won't
bring anything back. Trivial and
unoriginal, perchance, but true. Embrace
that excellent motto, catch the occasion!

Gradually cycles changed, flaws challenged
family gatherings demanded patience
monthlies stretched pain thresholds
fortnightly swimming - especially front crawl –
brought terrible cramp
grammaire française became taxing, scary
deutsche Grammatik enticed with strangeness
painting, charcoal drawing, sketching remained 'good'
claywork cracked after firing.
Friday disco-nights lacked handsome partners
gym handstands generally stayed sitting.
Each morning, and all precious girltime, repeating
helical DNA chains threaded then
rethreaded anti-parallel strands
creating proteins and translating
RNA transcripts into genetic tales
silently secreting an enigmatic watermark
ancient spelling mistake
framing relentless toxic destiny
spearheading eventual attacks
aimed at concealed unsuspecting vulnerable targets
instigating hereditary hurt

DNA Time

Molecules change, gyrating around
tight corners, describing
turns, joining paths, pairing
thymine, cytosine, guanine, adenine. Their
trajectories grow, glide, glisten,
trace orbits across the
planet's vaults, its
indigo ceilings, go past grandest spaces,
channel gravity. What force
urges adults to go and tackle
dilemmas that confusion compounds and mature
age multiplies? Imaginably the fact that - as
this DNA writing
clearly demonstrates through overlapping
intersecting constructs - all the potential riches
gained through living can generate poetry.

Green, lilac, scarlet raffia roughly plaited
forming bracelets, baskets, gaudy placemats
steps strung together decoded dances.
Dad swept spiralling woodshavings clear
stunning magenta dahlias cast cacti symmetry.
After choral chanting all the timestables
splashing each other with "… are sixty"
learning Friday wordlists (hardest definitely "Egypt")
night time's tepid bathwater trickled out,
sparkling scattered stars, craft landings and
Armstrong's moonwalks demanded avid attention
fancy aaas, italic ttts, time-consuming gallant gggs
took shape into phrases, ascribed meanings.
Shakespeare's glorious cadences, Hughes' landscapes
and Hardy's aching call struck receptive ears
with poetic ideas.

Fate, destiny, chance
(their outcomes concealed through subtle time
stratagems and secrets)
started far earlier than
conception. Chained backwords
the fabric that glues all
creatures through years, centuries, generations
reaches today and shapes
individuals. Grandparents, parents,
are serial, alternating puppet strings
(micro-, sub-conscious) dangling evolution's true children. Great
actors create characters, weak actors
imitate other actors' accents. Thus
descendants try their seemingly
innocent trick: copying their progenitors. Adolescents
question that ingrained instinct. Tolerate,
toughen-up? Complain, protest, reject? Balanced
amongst caring concerns,
forbearing anxieties, timid advances and
nagging insecurities needing encouragement,
the teenagers surface to
gasp their breath, ultimately grab independence

MARTIN HELPS OUT ON THE ALLOTMENT

Martin arrives via Lidl
changes his shoes on the patio
likes building up a quick sweat.

Martin pulls out stubborn bracken
attacks solid clumps of comfrey
turns over baked soil.

Martin clears up some 'bad' weeds
fears disturbing 'things that might be flowers'
dislikes picking blackcurrants.

Martin sips Earl Grey or lime cordial
talks poetry and the perils of Reading FC
takes home kale, chard or spinach for his tea.

AT CLIFF'S WORKSHOP

He teaches us to savour silences
let words breathe and flow
before we pour sounds on to paper
give them voice.

His silences frighten some
energise others to cut through
unnecessary interference
edge words
into better shape
ease them
into new possibilities.

UNSOLICITED

We're contacting you
about a personal injury claim
incurred through unfelt whiplash
during collision with an unseen delivery van
whose driver was answering an unknown call
re termination of a fictitious account
for non-payment of debts not owed.

FAST ANGER

After a very near miss
on the pelican crossing
your fast car flings open
driver's door
blocks the pavement
makes it hard
for those nearly hit to walk
by without clocking
slashed fabric interior
stashed with delivery boxes
dented bumper
smeared, shabby silver.

On our approach you
grab a parcel
loom by number 13's front door
big in an un-weeded garden
darkly clothed, hair
splayed under Nike cap
eyes not fully open
but following us
wanting to get ahead of a moment
bring it under control.

With a kick of invisible spurs
wag of index finger
you bristle with stubborn certainty
shout imaginary highway code
try to own
angry space.

GREEN ALKANET

You bear a name better suited
to a minor prog rock band
obscure brand of washing-up liquid,
foul tasting decongestant
or a wash for warts.

Unsung, lesser variant
your scratchy ubiquitous leaves
hard-to-get-rid-of tubers
amass in almost any soil.
Your sub forget-me eyes don't share
the kohl flicks of smokier azure cousins.

Infrequently visited by bees,
who rate you third choice after
boutique borage hotbeds
and dangling comfrey lay-bys,
you will always be a stopover
never a destination.

THE SLEEPERS IN THE HEDGE

Cast aside after their grand garden years
the sleepers in the hedge kneel in marble supplication
unaware of wren, blue tit and sparrow who flit in
and out of hawthorn much earlier
than before to salvage rubber bands,
plastic net or anything flexible that comes to beak.

The sleepers do not hear chiffchaffs herald
February spring, the song thrush call,
remain oblivious to toads hiding
croaks under hot April stones and have
no notion that hedgehog's scuffle grunt
long retreated into distant dreams.

The sleepers are senseless of July's
tinder-ripe leaves beneath their knees
have no taste memory of tart bilberries
creamy cobnuts, sloes fit for soaking in the fat autumns.
They have no idea how many fruits now fail
leaving our jam store empty.

The sleepers will never smell honeysuckle's
elegant fragrance entwining
along blackthorn prickle or heavy
Himalayan balsam wafting up stream
neither can they marvel at succulent hips
birds' winter feast shrivelled too soon.

The sleepers cannot see neighbouring
fields drying to dust or the wide river
thinning to a valley vein.
They have missed kingfisher's brilliant turquoise
red underwing's erratic night-time fluttering
but now, so do we all.

AMELANCHIER
i.m. Margaret Middleton

Once you tried to grow in the wrong place
didn't like the wind tunnel of an alley
that sent a chill to your roots.
You wanted to be somewhere else
not centre stage but in a space
where you could shelter from
frosts and sharp morning light
where mid-afternoon sun would comfort you
where you could hold your own
yet find companionship
where you might eventually blossom.

Now feathery white flowers dust early spring
darker leaves accentuate your slender beauty
contrast with powder red tulips beneath.
You'll be eclipsed soon by pink-flushed apple
fulsome pear, show-stopping lilac
but you'll grow on
steadfast, uncompromising.

WHAT BEFELL THEM
   (from: *Hammond's Book of Trees and Shrubs, 1909–1937*
   Hammond's Arboretum, Market Harborough)

Many were eaten by a heifer
pushing through, horses breaking
down fences in the dry season
or insects eating every leaf but one.

Vitus Inconstans had its main stem
mistakenly cut by Mr Buchanan.
Persimmon's head was knocked off
by a careless boy.

Comice Pear does not bear well:
many pears in the hot months
but all fell, attacked by wasps,
with little fruit since.

The Tree of Heaven reached 19ft 6
in 1922, rapid growth
amongst stunted trees
smothered by ivy and by weeds.

Minulus Harrisoni (Musk) is remarkable
for having, like all other specimens,
entirely lost its scent
since the period of the War.

TOAD'S AUTUMN ADVENTURE

Once summer's over
                Toad dozes
in a sack or shuffle-grunts
behind rake and spade
merging with greenhouse greenery.

This year, after a week-long nap
in a woollen hat, he leaves his shit behind
steps out from hibernation malarkey
hoping to live it up for once where
wide-eyed frogs lay in wait
for curvaceous snails, flies
oozing slugs and other slurp-ables.

Toad searches the water-butt side for a princess
or maybe a prince, to scoop him
out of his crusty stupor, yank him
off his haunches for a razzle dazzle among
crinkly kale, zazzing late nasturtiums

Soon
very soon
he could be giddy with kisses.

ON FIRE

We never leave the chip pan on high
pinch out candles at bedtime.

Tina's kids don't singe the lounge carpet
playing with indoor sparklers.

Allotment Barry douses his weekly bonfires
and Liz is wary with her weed burner.

Neither Harry's ciggies nor grandad's pipe
are left to smoulder in ashtrays.

Although she rushes out to work
Bina always unplugs her straighteners.

Rob, experimenting with Japanese wood burning,
does not let Albert fry ants with his magnifying glass.

Hope smothers embers fastidiously
while Woody is super cautious with forest picnics.

Oscar rarely overloads electric circuits
even when charging his appliances

and Michael definitely turned off his flame-retardant
Christmas tree lights before flying back to Patagonia.

So why is our house still burning?

THE CAMELLIA HOUSE

Closed for months
the Camellia House readies itself
to reveal spirograph patterned
vulnerable would-be roses

but frosts nip beauty in bud.
Soft pink, blistering coral
unlabelled cream and yellow blooms
brown over in bitter cold.

She waits, well wrapped-up,
on their bench nearest the ha-ha
catches snatches of chat
from infrequent golfers on the twelfth.

They've always been careful
to use different car parks.

He usually breezes in
on the brick path funnelled by
ancient firs, brooding yew
dark into light.

She is not alone today.
By the entrance a couple bicker
about breast-feeding times
wonder if baby will ever calm down.

A photographer tests out settings
paces among bare flowerbeds
irritated by walkers popping in
and out of his shot.

She peers through an open door
glimpses nothing but once shiny leaves
crisping at their edges
dead petals.

HOLIDAY VILLAGE

Old Granary
Old Tannery
Old Bakery

Old Stables

Old Brewhouse
Old Schoolhouse
Old Boat House

Old Cowshed

Old Rectory
Old Surgery
Old Joinery

Old Smithy

Old Farmhouse
Old Coal House
Old Lighthouse

Old Pig Pen

SCOPUS OWL, MALLORCA

I thought it was your scowl squeal I heard
two evenings ago out there
somewhere on the starry black mountainside
beyond the cypress trees
but here you are now, in front of me,
stuffed, stitched and labelled behind glass.
So much smaller than I expected
given the way you split
open the night sky's silences.

NAVIGATING HALF-SLEEP

At first you keep all at bay
wallowing in half-slumber
but then morning's noises
radiator tick, distant thrum
and hum of ring road traffic
builders climbing roof scaffold
wind stirring in soon-to-be naked
apple trees seep inwards, dredging
across edges of dreams.
leaving you – ready or not –
fully landed.

Five thousand kilometres still to go
a bar-tailed godwit high above
alternates between one part of her brain
and the other. Fully operational
with one closed eye she navigates
storms and surges of open ocean.
Half in deep-sleep on the wing
she knows where she is
and will arrive at the same estuary,
same breeding ground, same time as usual
where he will land
synchronously.

JUNIOR SICK BAY

1970s
Pillows cocooned you from British Bulldog rampage
hopscotch count skip and leap. Teachers' tea breaks
murmured through an adjacent wall
before a whistle shrilled each playground
squabble into class-ready straightness.

The Sick Bay was a holding space for Mr. Quangle
Wangle's hat, a folded pea-green boat
maypole ribbons, tinfoil wings, a lamp in need of a shine.
Its zig-zag bed was less sturdy than your own.
Rough red blankets covered gingham
trutex, gaberdine. Only sensible shoes, blazer
and, sometimes, tie were ever removed
as you feigned illness or sleep, missed perfecting
italic *fffs*, cross-stitching your bianca dressing table set
in slow afternoons before school's end
when you would walk home unaided.

2020s
Now there's a cold shell
of a room, a wide open window
yellow-black warning signs
shelves full of out-of-bounds boxes.

She watches through mask and visor
to be sure nothing is touched.
Her plastic apron rustles, mobile beeps
but you must sit still, stay silent
wait for the test's tell-tale lines
and someone to collect you.

ACROSS COLNE WATER

A season concertinas into
wheezy tears and sirens
choking magpies, wrens
in full hedgerow throttle.

Black cows munch velvet hillside.
Scattered sheep huddle
close to the leeward brow
of a drystone wall.

Kestrels hover and wait, crows
with sealed beaks watch
two girls steer their rainbow kite
through thickening skies.

NOVEMBER THANKS

Thanks to soft Autumn
easing through sycamore and oak
haloing our heads as we walk
across frost-thawed grass.

Thanks to the couple who watch
their girls scoop handfuls of leaves
throw them over each other repeat
in a muddy flurry of giggles.

Thanks to Van Jones for his tears
on CNN for his Muslim family
for friends who can breathe more
easily, sleep less fearfully.

Thanks to the beeches for their slow
releasing bounty which scuds
and skitters and scatters
on a Sherwood twilight street.

Thanks to this day.

OUT OF TIME

One March day streets peeled away
in a rear memory mirror as the world
shrunk to us and our back garden.
On the second day I was forbidden
to take pets I didn't have
for an imaginary walk so I strolled
along allotment back lanes
spying nude mannequins
sparrows in nestbuilding fervour.
Tearful people flicked switches
on new time. Lucky ones opened
a portal through worked soil, shared stories
of late frosts, signs their seeds were growing.
Somebody said sun cream
might help or was it paracetamol?
On the tenth day actors stood too
close in *A Fish Called Wanda*.
They hugged and chatted and fought
while little dogs got caught in the crossfire.
On day thirteen I should have
packed an overnight bag
had my medication ready
but on day thirteen and a half
I turned off notifications.
By day nineteen fringes were flowing
over noses, beards caused accidents
postwomen in summer shorts struggled
with greedy parcels down empty streets.
On the twenty-eighth day footballs
missed their goals, running tracks melted
swimming pools ran dry and swings hung lifeless.
On the thirty-second day politicians
polished their falsehoods

windows spontaneously opened and shut
applause flickered across hawthorn
to the accompaniment of urgent wrens.
On day thirty-seven Teams broke up
Houseparties squabbled, Zooms
ploughed into slow lanes.
On the fortieth day pavements
longed for the press of feet
echoes of laughter, snails prayed
for a slick of loud rain, yearned to smear
their fresh paths across silent sunshine.

SPRING LEARNING

(I)

We overschedule our days on
shared screens, heads disappearing
into false places. Encircled faces
unseen behind initials. Voices are switched on
or muted. Conversations become concentrated.
Staccato chat replaces warm chatter
with hard-to-read silences punctuated
by emojis, fixing and unfixing smiles.
Tears flow, virtual hands go up or
stay down but are rarely tentative,
spontaneous, waving.

(II)

Outside in a bright spring fluffed-up blue tits
negotiate the evening birdbath queue for
their place in a pecking order behind loud sparrow brood.
A young blackbird's saffron-rimmed eye queries
what might be seeds before he bounces off to
learn to bend his worm-listening head lawn-wards.
Fledgling robins flit back-forth between
turned soil and sheltered hawthorn territory.
A glow of speckles, needy yellow beaks yearning
red breasts not earned yet. Later a hidden tawny owl
haunts pear tree dark, waits for a possible
mate's echo, sends a shiver through
pre-dawn with her unexpected hooting.

JUNE '19 OVER CON-FUSION

In the stickiness of a hot
wet day when there's no fruit left on the buffet
a peculiar milkshake explodes coffee
over whipped cream over
cold froth over chocolate sprinkles
over plastic lid over
plastic cup over narrow counter
over uniformed milkshake maker
who curses and starts the sickly
shake making all over again.

In the overheated carriage
an unreliable narrator mixes
Hitchcock with Du Maurier
tricks us right till the end of his story
a bloody bumbling politician
who skips and quips and ducks
and dives and fucks with other people's futures.

'You should have gone the other way'
someone shouts.
Gone over the path
with dark displaced toads
over the kerb through a rarely opened gate
taxi-ing on to hallowed ground at the Radcliffe Road End
with an Indian outpatient grandmother
and her tiny scooter
and her big ticket
flying to the crease to catch
England
India

Bangladesh
Sri Lanka
Pakistan.

An excitable passenger on the Derby train
screams at a minute mobile screen
as his team's overs tick by.
Yes, you should have gone the other way round!
Shortened your trousers.
Shortened your lists.
Not taken your bicycle
over groomed green lawns
out in to the park
where none can be seen
whether ridden or pushed.

RAW COUNTRY

Out into raw country where bare hedges
burnished by winter sun blaze in defiance

before darkness, three crows
squabble kerbside over a squashed vixen

her white tail tip still distinct from
the bloodied rest of her rusty body

and blackbirds throw their last-light songs from
bold oaks along a pinking skyline as

cold creeps, grips, hardens on
field edges and plough turns once more.

WHEN WILL THE ROBIN WILL COME?

When she's good and ready
and you have turned over enough earth
to make it worth her while in worms.

HIDING PLACES

While she counts to a hundred
through a veil of red fingers

you are breathing red velvet
behind the stairway curtain
soaking up living-room murmurs of aunts
pretending they don't know where you are.

Or you are crouching behind Dad's shed
among water-butt toads and stinky compost,
mossy window frames and waving branches
outstaring next door's ever curious cat.

Or you are squeezing between heavy-scented lilac
and your playhouse window
trying not to give the game away
with your reflection in the glass.

Or you are flattening against the house wall
beyond where the chimney breast juts out,
fingers reddening with brick dust
risking the hellos of nosy neighbours.

Or you are scrunching inside the airing cupboard
arms tight round the water tank
stifling giggles and whispers
among warm fluff and watery gurgles.

Or you are curling under the spare bed
in the space the Hoover never reaches
among lost toys and magazines,
dolls' legs and silent dust.

You must not move
even though your nose is tickling,
your foot is itching,
your breath is trembling.

Any minute now
she could come creeping
near
nearer
and find you.

HITCHERS, CUBA

Everyday along the highway
there's the same routine
a crumpled dollar in a workman's hand;
an offer of fruit – orange, mango, banana.
I'll be your eyes one woman says
but we take nothing
save their knowledge of the road.

They work lifts for each other,
transitions quickly negotiated
a smile, a hand pointed in the right
direction, a nod confirming safety.

Some exchange names, places, situations
but the next three in line are strangers
hesitant, holding fast to possessions
a net of avocados, a kitbag, a stethoscope.
An old soldier makes no eye contact for hours
but mouths *gracias* on leaving,
his place already taken.

Others shake hands, depart with a rush
send us on our way with advice,
their hands forming roundabouts
elbows show crossroads
forearms become unmarked tracks
Directo! Directo!

At the roadside, old men stand with poles of onions,
packets of tamarind. Women rush towards the car,
stroking pet bunches of bananas.
A young man hides behind a bus shelter,
scurries forward once a girl gets him a ride.

Some sleep off their shifts in air-conditioned comfort:
a big guy in Sunday best, a sweating labourer,
fruit pickers with rosy papayas
all wake suddenly
fearful of missed destinations.

One couple entrust us
with grandma and daughter.
Their girl is all fidget
pulls up her socks, crinkles then smoothes
clothes, rustles her bag before being shushed
by grandma who shrinks herself
into a tiny space but keeps her eyes alive
ready to save us all from tracks
to nowhere, back roads that slip in to the sea.

Juan, a chef, tears up guavas. Their pink flesh,
thick pips leave a lingering sweet-sourness.
He knows the road, each pothole and crater,
tight bend and narrowing section.
He winces when lorries almost scrape
bodywork or we swerve deep ruts in the highway.

Juan answers almost all our questions
knows about soaring turkey vultures
their dark wings casting
huge serrated shadows.
He could find local bays and secret
swimming places, juicy lobster and camarones,
statues of heroes of the revolution.
We know he has been visiting his son
and will work late in his brother's parador tonight.
We know what he thinks of our itinerary,
our hotel, the cocktails they'll serve on our arrival
but we will never discover what he thinks of us
outsiders, travelling how and when we choose.

STAFF-STUDENT COMMITTEE ROOM, AUTUMN 1983

The committee room wasn't cold
but was unwelcoming.

The leatherette writing pads were
not real leather, pencils rested
almost at right angles and glasses
failed to sparkle with fresh water.

You weren't well dressed that day.
Tired leather jacket, People's March for Jobs
t-shirt heading toward disposal.

The committee members showed
no sympathy. Did they even hear your
apology for lateness or take in the bit
about your mangled bike, your lucky escape?

No-one else found you a seat.
No-one else saw the shiver.
There was no other outward sign.

Sun never filtered through half-closed
blinds to frame us in an ethereal glow.

You didn't know I would reach
for your hand. Neither did I.

I didn't know, not at first,
that you would take me off
in a new direction, one I was unclear
I wanted to go in.

I didn't know then your love
would hold me like this.

WIND WANDERER

You have gone to walk in the wind my love
along paths that are tinder dry
among scratchy leaves of summer's end
and fennel flowers shoulder high.

You have gone to walk in the wind my love
where greedy donkeys roam
lizards skid-addle over the escarpment
and goats bleat far from home.

You have gone to walk in the wind my love
in the long hot afternoon
when cicadas grind rusty engines
and linnets sing hidden tunes.

You have gone to walk in the wind my love
to think and drift into dreams
where swallowtails flex their colours
and shadows chase over the chênes.

You have gone to walk in the wind my love
up where short-toed eagles soar
and finches string their golden charms
while darkness waits for the wild boar.

You have gone to walk in the wind my love
because you always need to stray
but your heart rests here with me my love.
I would not have it any other way.

INSTRUCTIONS FOR A FRIEND

Take stock
leave clocks to their own ticking
unlock your door to new daylight.

Seek rest
don't test yourself every second
save your best moments for dreaming.

ACKNOWLEDGEMENTS

Sue wished to thank Melbourne UNESCO City of Literature for her virtual residency at the Victoria State Library and Inspire Libraries, Nottinghamshire for facilitating the *Poetry Place* exhibition, book and workshops. 'Becoming Silver Birch', 'Hawk on the Window Ledge' and 'Leaving Party' first appeared in a privately circulated 'Eyelet' pamphlet *Five Poems*, published by Shoestring Press in 2017. 'Wakes Outings', 'Our Bestwood Picnic' and 'Questions for Postcard Photographers' first appeared in *Poetry Place*. We thank the Inspire Picture Archive for permission to reproduce the accompanying photographs. Other poems in this collection first appeared in Raceme, Spelt, English in Education, Dreich, London Grip and the University of Wisconsin Covid anthology *Sheltering with Poems*. 'Hiding Places' was first published in *I Remember, I Remember* ed Brian Moses, 2003, Macmillan Children's Books.

'Out of Time' first appeared in Ohio State University's digital anthology *Dwelling during the Pandemic*. Sue's reading of 'Mobile' can still be heard on the *Dial-a-Poem* app (2020), a project led by Nottingham Trent University and funded by the Arts and Humanities Research Council. Dial 3280. 'First Blood' was written for a short film first shown at Nottingham Playhouse on National Poetry Day in 2019. It can be seen at https://suedymokepoetry.com/2019/10/03/first-blood-a-poem-film-for-national-poetry-day-2/